volcano
vegetables
V
vulture
violin
vacuum cleaner
vase

v for volcano

v for vulture

v for **v**iolin

v for **v**acuum cleaner

v for vase

v for **v**egetables
I love to eat

The **v**ulture eats
between his meals, and
that's the reason why
he **v**ery **v**ery rarely feels
as well as you and I.